China

Your Ultimate Guide to Traveling, Culture, History, Food and More!

By Asha Miyazaki

Experience Everything Travel Guide Collection™

EXPERIENCE
EVERYTHING
P U B L I S H I N G

Forward

Thank you for purchasing this book from the Experience Everything Travel Guide Collection™! Inside you will find a ton of useful, informative and entertaining information on China and it is our desire that this book will provide you with the inspiration to explore!

Disclaimer

While this book contains a great deal of information, it does not have all of the information that is available on the Internet. It is written to inspire you about the destination rather than act as a full travel guide that you could use to get from point A to point B or to specific addresses/locations during your tour.

This document is geared towards providing exact and reliable information in regards to the topic and issue covered. The publication is sold with the idea that the publisher is not required to render accounting, officially permitted, or otherwise, qualified services. If advice is necessary, legal or professional, a practiced individual in the profession should be ordered.

- From a Declaration of Principles which was accepted and approved equally by a Committee of the American Bar Association and a Committee of Publishers and Associations:

The information herein is offered for informational purposes solely, and is universal as so. The presentation of the information is without contract or any type of guarantee assurance.

Introduction

China has been regarded as the land of the sleeping giant. This may be because of the the country's tremendous population. Take note that China is the most populated country in the world and their language, Chinese, is spoken almost anywhere in the world too!

Apart from the many inhabitants of this country, there are a lot of great places to visit, exquisite and exotic food to taste and a rich history and culture to unravel. You will find it exciting to take part of their customs and traditions while visiting the country. You can also discover your luck by going to a fortune teller. Visitors can also try their renowned herbal medicines and alternative therapy and wellness programs.

The country has more than 4000 years of civilization. It is no wonder that many westerners including Marco Polo has been fascinated with the country's heritage and its people. Moreover, the people in the country have been taught English in the past 20 years. This has been mandatory from late elementary until middle school. It has also been a requirement to be able to obtain a degree in university. This means that visitors will be able to communicate with the locals as most of them have basic English skills.

Visitors who want to visit China can fly in Beijing, Guangzhou and Shanghai airports. You can even fly in from Hong Kong for a holiday trip to the country. Take note that those who wish to enter the country can even have a train ride all the way from Europe. Russia and Europe railways offer train rides going to Beijing while Kazakstan and Central Asia also provide train rides. Other trips by train are also available from Hong Kong, North Korea and Vietnam. Once you embark for a journey to China, you may get surprised that you are actually enjoying the country and their culture and may even settle for good!

Chapter I: Geography

Highlands, Peaks, Rivers and Drainage

The tallest mountains in the world divides the country from the Central and Southern parts of Asia. This includes the Karakorum, Tian Shan, Himalayas and the Pamirs. In the Himalayas, you will be able to find the world's tallest peak, Mt. Everest. Meanwhile, K2, the second highest mountain, is also found in the country bordering Pakistan. Nine others out of the 17 tallest peaks in the world are also found in China. You will also find the Tibetan Plateau in the country just east of the Pamirs and Karakorum. It covers 2.5 million square kilometers or about 1/5 of the total land area of the country.

On the western borders of China lies nine other tallest peaks including Lhotse, Cho Oyu, Gyachung Kang, Gasherbrum II, Makalu, Broad Peak, Gasherbrum III and Gasherbrum IV. Within the country lies the Namchabarwa and Shishapangma mountains. Outside the Himalayas, you will be able to find tallest peaks including Muztagh Ata, Kongur Tagh, Gongga Shan and Tomur Shan.

There are about 50,000 rivers found in China with more than 100 sq. Kilometers of catchment area. More than one thousand of these rivers have a catchment area over 1,000 sq. Kilometers. Meanwhile, the total length of these rivers is at 420,000 kilometers with majority of its flow reaching the Pacific Ocean.

In Tibet, the Yangtze river's length measures 6,300 kilometers and flows entering the East China Sea. The total catchment area of the river measures 1.8 million square kilometers and ranks as the world's third longest river following the Amazon and the Nile. Meanwhile, the second longest river in the country is the Yellow River, Huang He, with a catchment area of 752,000 sq. Kilometers. You can also find the Black Dragon River, Pearl River, Liaohe River, Haihe River, Qiantang River, Pearl River Delta and the Lancang River.

Many of these rivers in the country dry up in the desert or flow into lakes. Some of these are used of irrigation as agriculture is also China's top industry. The waters in the country are actually marginal seas to Pacific Ocean's western part.

China Regions and Cities

The official name of China is the "People's Republic of China". It is about as big as the United States in terms of geographical site and lies in the Eastern Asia region. This huge country is also the border of 14 other countries including North Korea, Pakistan, Afghanistan, Kazakhstan, Russia, Mongolia, Tajikistan and Kyrgyzstan.

Meanwhile, the Yellow Sea, East China Sea, South China Sea and the Korea Bay are within the coasts of the country.

China has a total land area of 9.6 million km² and ranks third biggest country in terms of size after Russia and Canada. The country has been divided into 5 regions including Xinjiang-Mongolia, Highlands of Tibet and the Eastern China, with subdivisions including northeastern plain, southern hills and the north plain.

Discovering Regions around China

The northeastern part of China is composed of Jilin, Heilongjiang and Liaoning. These are mostly old cities with large forests, experiencing long snowy winters. The people in this region have been largely influenced by the Japanese, Koreans and Russians.

Meanwhile, the northern China region is made up of Inner Mongolia, Henan, Hebei, Shandong, Shanxi, Tianjin and Beijing. The area is referred to as the Yellow River Basin because it serves as China's cradle for civilization. It is also regarded as the place holding most of the country's rich history. The northwest Chinese region is composed of Gansu, Xinjiang, Shaanxi, Qinghai and Ningxia provinces. This is also the site that holds the capital of the country 1000 years ago. It is made up of mostly dessert and grasslands where people are mostly nomads and Islam believers.

In the southwest China region, a backpacker haven where spectacular scenery lies awaits visitors. It is composed of the provinces of Guizhou, Guangxi, Tibet and Yunnan. Going to south central China, you will be able to find Chongqing, Hunan, Jiangxi, Sichuan, Anhui and Hubei provinces. This region holds mountainous areas, river gorges as well as farmlands. The region has subtropical forests with temperate climates. Provinces of Fujian, Guangdong and Hainan are found in southeast China where traditional trading centers can be found. You will be able to see manufacturing industries in this area.

Meanwhile, the provinces of Zhejiang, Jiangsu and Shanghai are found in the eastern China region. The region has been referred to as the land of rice and fish as this is China's newest cosmopolitan economic center.

Top Cities in China

There are many cities to visit while spending a holiday trip in China. These cities vary in sizes, population and attractions. You will be able to experience a touch of magic and wonder while touring around the country, visiting famous spots and enjoying a variety of culture and ethnicity.

Take a trip to China's capital, Beijing, to experience the cultural center. You can also head on to Guangzhou, the country's most liberal city, just south of

Hong Kong. For those who love to go mountain climbing and those who adore great river scenes, going to Guilin is a must. Meanwhile, you can also visit Hangzhou, regarded as the most beautiful city in the country, and look around for their intricate silk products.

You can also take a trip to Yunnan's capital, Kunmin, and enjoy ethnic diversity. The historical and cultural city of Nanjing is also best for those who want to travel back to history. Go shopping in te city of Shanghai while enjoying the riverside views within the area. Travelers can also visit the Venice of the East, Suzhou, where they would be able to find hanging gardens and ancient cities with canals.

The infamous terracotta warriors and the Silk Road can be found in Xi'an, which is also the oldest city of the country. It was once the capital of China and holds the Tang and Han dynasties and eight others. Another history filled city to visit is Yangzhou where Marco Polo has been governor during the 13th century. The city is also filled with more than 2,500 years of history and has been referred to as the epitome of the country.

Types of Visas for Your China Trip

Like many other countries, visitors intending to enter China will need to obtain a visa. You can apply for this in a Chinese embassy in your country before your planned departure. There are many types of visa offered to foreigners who want to go to the country. Meanwhile, those coming from Western countries are exempted from securing a visa when visiting Macau and Hong Kong. Citizens of Singapore, Brunei and Japan do need to secure a visa when visiting mainland China. They are given 15 days of stay regardless of their purpose to visit. Meanwhile, nationals coming from San Marino are given up to 90 days of stay regardless of reason when visiting the country.

Getting a tourist visa is not as difficult compared to a working or business visa for a planned trip to China. Usually, you will be entitled to a 1 month stay in the country for a single-entry visa to be used within 3 months from the date when it was issued. Meanwhile, tourists who are able to secure a double-entry tourist visa are allowed to have it used within 6 months from the date of issue. Tourist visas are also issued for citizens of some countries allowing the a total of 3 months stay while in China.

Chapter II: China's History and Culture

China's civilization was said to have started in the Yellow River. The first dynasty to be established in the country was the Xia Dynasty according to ancient chronicles although there was no concrete evidence found of its existence. However, archaeologists found out that there was indeed a civilization developed during the described period.

Meanwhile, the first confirmed dynasty of China was the Shang Dynasty followed by the Zhou Dynasty that ruled across the basin of the Yellow River. The Zhou Dynasty, the longest ruling dynasty in the history of the country, developed their own goverent system and ruled the territories using feudal lords.

By 221 BC, the country was unified under its first emperor, Qin Shi Huang during the Qin Dynasty. Emperor Qin instituted the centralization of the government system. The ideals of this system is still strongly adapted even in modern day China.

After 15 long years of the Qin Dynasty, the Han Dynasty took over by 206 BC, regarded as the golden age of the country's civilization. After the dynasty collapsed in 220 CE, the three kingdoms period succeed where the country was put into political chaos and war leading to a split of the country into Shu, Wei and Wu states.

The country was briefly reunited under the Jin Dynasty before being divided into anarchy once more and ended following the Sui period 581. By 1911, the imperial system running for 2000 years collapsed after Sun Yat Sen established the Republic of China. In 1919, the May Fourth Movement was established which paved the way for the reorganization of the Koumintang and the Chinese Communist Party.

Understanding China's Cultural Diversity

The country has diverse culture, customs and even language. The economic levels also vary from one city to another. For instance, Guangzhou, Shanghai and Beijing are more economically stable and wealthy. Meanwhile, 50% of the population are still living the rural areas even as there is only very little arable land. Some of them use animals and do manual labor to sustain daily needs while former peasants have already moved to cities and other neighboring towns in search for work.

According to government data, there are about 90 million people who earn less than Y924 annually. Meanwhile, the same data said there were about 26 million people who are below poverty line earning only Y668 per year. Generally, the eastern and the coastal regions in the south are regarded wealthy while those in inland areas, north, southwest and those from the far west are considered less developed.

Despite the size of China, you would be surprise to see the diversity of its cultural landscape. There are a total of 56 ethnic groups that are officially recognized by the government. The biggest group among these is the Hans, constituting more than 90% of the total population of the country. Meanwhile, other ethnic groups are exempted from the one child policy of the country and almost positive responses from university admissions.

These minority ethnic groups have their own language. The culture in China share common elements but there is no unified belief. Deities and customs differ from one village to another. National festivals and the celebration of the Chinese new year also vary in different regions of the country. Weddings and funerals are also celebrated differently depending on the ethnic group. In general, the culture of the Chinese people is a combination of traditional and secular.

Normal behaviors in China That May Be Disturbing To Foreigners

There are a lot of behaviors displayed by the people in China that may be disturbing to foreigners as it may seem unethical or out of the ordinary. This includes public spitting since they believe that swallowing your phlegm is unhealthy. They would spit on the streets, in shops, hotel lobbies and even in supermarkets. In developed areas like Shanghai and Beijing, spitting has declined especially when the SARS epidemic broke out in 2002.

Smoking is also rampant in the country and you can find people smoking almost everywhere even in places bearing no smoking signs. Some establishments do not even provide ashtrays resulting to cigarette butts thrown anywhere. If you don't smoke or prefer not to inhale or smell cigarette smoke, it would be wise to have a mask worn.

For those who don't have Chinese appearance, you should get used when people started calling out "laowai" at you. This is the colloquial term used to refer to a foreigner. This can happen several times a day from any person regardless of age whenever they see a foreigner. Discrimination to those having dark skin is also a common issue in China.

Aside from repeated acts of calling a foreigner several times a day, staring is also common. They would stare at you out of curiosity and not being hostile. Don't be surprised if a stranger comes to you just to stare as you look different from the rest of them. Loud conversation and noise even in public places is also common. They would talk very loud even in the early hours of the morning.

Sanitation is another issue in China. Many of the people blow their nose in public without covering as well as coughing disregarding the person in front of them. It is also common for small kids to urinate or poop in public places.

Chinese Belief on Numbers

China, over the years, has believed in fortune tellers, cards, astrology and even magic. They also believe in getting lucky by following numbers in pattern. For most of them, the numbers 3, 6, 8 and 9 signifies luck. They also believe that the number three means it is shining above the three stars. The number six, according to them, indicates success resulting to a number of weddings held on dates with 6. Meanwhile, the number eight is regarded to be closely attached to prosperity and wealth.

While there are lucky numbers, there are also those that are deemed unlucky. For most of them, the number four is a taboo since it sounds like "death" when spoken in Mandarin. Most of their hotels do not have fourth floors comparable to the unlucky 13th of the Americans.

Religion in China

The most number of Chines practice Buddhism. It is believed that the religion was indoctrinated in 67 AD in the country during the reign of the Han Dynasty from Xinjiang to Central China. The development of the religion has influenced the people's thoughts in culture and tradition. It has also become among the most important religions in the country during that time.

There are three different Buddhist religions that evolved in the country. The diverse ethnicity of the people has also affected the way the religion was developed and practiced. Later on, these religions became the Tibetan, Han and the Southern Buddhism. Today, temples as well as Buddhist caves have become major tourist spots.

Aside from Buddhism, other people in the country also practice Taoism, which means the thought or the way of life. It was developed through the influence of Lao Tzu during the 6th century BC.

Chapter III: Modes of Transportation in China

There are different transportation systems in China that you can choose from. For international and domestic travels, you can book a trip by plane. You can also ride buses, trains, taxis and even rent cars. Ferries and boats are also available as well as bicycle rides.

The fare also vary depending on which transportation system you use. It would also depend upon the distance of the place where you will be heading to. You also have to take note of the season of your travel as travel peak seasons also have higher fare prices.

Traveling By Plane

If you are coming abroad, gateway of mainland China is in Beijing, Guangzhou and Shanghai. Some cities also have airports but only cater to international flights coming from Japan, South Korea and some countries from Southeast Asia. Some Asian air carriers with flights to China include Korean Air, Cathay Pacific, Singapore Airlines, Garuda Indonesia and Japan Airlines.

Currently, there are a lot of major airlines flying to China through Guangzhou, Beijing and Shanghai. However, you will find very few budget fares for these flights that is why it is good to have a flight booked earlier. Tickets go high by the start and end of the summer season.

This is because most students come home from abroad and would go back after their vacation. Tickets also increase in prices during the approach of the Chinese New Year.

Getting A Train Ride To China

Visitors coming in from neighboring countries can conveniently take the train. Those coming even from Europe can visit the country by getting a train ride. From Russia and Europe, you can choose from Trans-Siberian Railway lines. The train will run from Moscow to Beijing with several stops from cities in Russia in between the time of travel.

The northwestern province of Xinjiang can be reached from Kazakhstan and Central Asia also by taking a train ride. However, custom checkups can cause long waits as well as having wheelbase changed for the track of the next country.

Hong Kong and mainland China are connected by regular train rides. However you have to ensure you have the appropriate visa because immigration checkups will be done after reaching the border. You can also travel from Vietnam going to China by train through the Friendship Pass.

However, trips coming from Kunming were canceled since 2002. Another train ride can be taken from North Korea to Beijing and operates four times a week.

Trains are classified according to their speed. G-series trains travel at the speed of 300 km per hour. The routes are from Guangzhou to Wuhan, Beijing to Xi'an, Shanghai to Hangzhou, Zhengzhou to Xi'an, Guangzhou to Shenzhen, Haerbin to Dalian and Beijing to Shanghai.

Meanwhile, the C-series trains travel short haul and high speed expresses with a speed of 300 km per hour. The D-series travel at 200 km per hour in high speed express ways. The Z-series trains are non-stop trains connecting most of the country's major cities at the speed of 160 km per hour. It offers soft sleeper or soft seat accommodation with some hard sleepers as well.

You can also take the T-series trains having a speed of 140 km per hour and take the intercity routes. These are also similar to Z-trains but have more stops in most stations it come across. Another train you can take are the K-series trains running at 120 km per hour with more seats and hard sleepers on board.

There are also general fast trains and the general trains. The general fast trains run at 120 km per hour. The fare prices are the cheapest yet are also the slowest when it comes to long distance travels. On the other hand, the general trains are even slower, traveling 100 km per hour for short distance destinations. These trains stop almost everywhere and may not be a good option if you are on the rush.

Then there are soft sleeper and hard sleeper trains. Soft sleepers are those that allow you to comfortably sleep in four bunk compartments. These trains are made according to western standards and offer relatively cheaper rates. The bunks come with latched doors to give passengers privacy. Meanwhile, the hard sleepers have 3 beds in every column. Those who are as tall as 6'3" will find this comfortable as you can have your feet extended without getting bumped. Contrary to popular belief, hard sleepers don't have hard beds. It has a soft mattress to sleep on and can give you comfort while on board.

Tickets for a Train Ride

Tickets can be bought a week before your scheduled train ride. It is necessary that you make an advance purchase as bigger towns and wider routes often run out of tickets. Often times, you can get the "standing" class ticket when there few tickets left for sale. If you have bought this kind of ticket and wish to transfer to sleepers or seats, you can ask the conductor from time to time for availability.

As of 2002, foreigners who wish to take the train transportation should present an ID. Nationals are also required to do the same. You will need to present an identification card to be able to pickup your train ticket which indicates your name on it.

You can purchase tickets in advance by contacting a local ticket agencies. These railway ticket agents have their offices marked with "Booking Office for Train Tickets" signages, making it easier for you to identify where to go and make a purchase.

Road Trip To China

The country is bordered with 14 many other countries making it easier to travel by road. China's neighbor on its north is Russia while Macau and Hong Kong can also ge gateways using its special administrative regions. These roads are regarded as international borders due to their practical purpose.

A road trip to China can be tiring but very rewarding as well. You will be rewarded with majestic sceneries along the way as you pass remote mountain roads. Most of the roads you will take are crossings to China's west. Here you will find breathtaking views that will make you enjoy your road trip even more.

Bus Rides Around China

Traveling short distance places or within the city areas are best done through public city buses. These are cheaper rides with plastic seats. However, there are no English signs on board and you can't expect the driver to help you get to your destination. Meanwhile, if you know your route, then a bus ride can be a great transportation mode.

For long distance places, you can take the coaches. However, they can either be very comfortable for your traveling experience or otherwise. These buses are equipped with air conditioners with sleepers and soft seats. The roads taken by the coaches are smooth that will allow travels marvel scenic spots. The bus personnel can also assist you but most of them know very little English. Some of these coaches are equipped with a toilet that can be very dirty and uncomfortable especially when the bus takes a turn and water starts to splash.

Like trains, buses also have different types. The most common bus in the country are the sleeper buses. They have bunk beds instead of having seats of passengers. It is a good choice when you are traveling overnight. The bus runs at 100 km per hour along the freeway but may not be as comfortable for those who are tall or overweight.

In some places in the country, you will need to remove your shoes before getting in the bus. A personnel will provide you with a plastic bag to conveniently store your footwear. You can have it put on whenever a bus stops at a restaurant.

Enjoying the Subway

Subways are also another mode of transportation while in the country. These are often used by major cities including Shanghai, Beijing, Wuhan, Shenyang, Chengdu, Shenzhen and Nanjing.

You can get a ticket from machines that have signs written in Chinese and English. Most of the subways are under expansion construction to get major cities closely linked to one another. According to government data, China will soon have the most extensive urbanized transport system by 2020.

Woooot!! Taxi!

Travelers can also hail a cab to get around a city while spending their holidays in China. Taxi fares are reasonable that can range from Y5 to Y14 depending on which city you are. The succeeding kilometers are then charged Y2 but an ordinary trip can cost you around Y10 to Y50. Meanwhile, in other cities, fares can be more expensive especially when you travel at night. Finding a cab during peak hours can be very difficult too or when its raining hard. Aside from that, you will find it rather easier to find a cab. Some drivers would even offer you a 10% discount especially when you made an advance call with them. Furthermore, taxi drivers don't usually expect to be given tips but you can always do so if you wish.

Some travelers report that they have been cheated by a taxi driver over high fares while in China. However, cases recorded are very minimal and should not raise alarm. On the other hand, if you feel that the price you are being charged for a taxi fare is overly high, you can always ask your hotel's doorman or officer to assist you with the matter.

If this is your first time going to the country, you should also beware of hawkers operating inside or outside the airports. They would bargain with you taxi fares that you thought are cheap only to find out later that you have been charged 2x or even 3x higher than what you are supposed to pay.

Trams, Bicycles, Rickshaws and Motorcycles

Other transportation modes while in the country are trolleys otherwise known as the trams. This kind of transportation are often found in cities including Changchun and Dalian. However, they can get jammed in traffic but they can also offer you a good way of getting a city tour.

A bicycle ride is also a convenient way to get around the city. These are also the most common form of transportation in the country. During rush hours, you will see bikes flocking the streets almost everywhere. Most of these bicycles are traditional with single speed roadsters. However, modern day bikes have also become common nowadays.

Tourists can enjoy riding a bike than getting stuck in traffic. However, it can also be dangerous especially that most vehicles tend to pull over without giving signals. Theft is also rampant so you have to be careful where you park your bicycles. Of course, you wouldn't want to pay for the entire bike plus rent the moment it gets stolen.

In rural areas and smaller cities, you will find a lot of motorcycle taxis. Fares come cheap but rides can be scary. This is because some drivers don't have licenses and drive like they're on highway to hell. Most of the cities in the country have motorcycle markets offering cheap deals. However, you have to be careful about making a purchase because some of these motorcycles are illegally registered and have fake plates.

Meanwhile, the rickshaw, or pedicabs, can also be taken when you are in mid-sized cities. This is very ideal for those who want to travel short distance places. You can also negotiate the fare for a ride in advance to get the best deals with the driver.

If you decided to take a rickshaw ride, be careful not to halt those wearing traditional costumes as these drivers are usually reported to loot passengers. They can charge you ten times the regular fares compared to those normal looking drivers who can take you to the nearest subway at normal rates. Take note that whenever you ride a rickshaw, you are also helping poor families keep their businesses. Aside from that, you are also helping preserving one of the traditional transport system of the country.

Getting Around By Car

Going around China by car has some ups and downs. You need to be over 18 years old and must have a Chinese license to be able to do so. Remember that the country does not allow foreign licenses or even those issued in Hong Kong or Macau. Unless you have diplomatic status, there is no way you would be able to drive in China.

If you are planning to rent a car while in a China holiday, you don't need to worry about driving as a driver comes along with the deal. The downside of this is that roads are always jammed with traffic and you will find it difficult to get a parking place. There are also English signs that are erroneously written in most of the cities in the country making it more difficult for foreigners.

Chapter IV: Where to Stay While In China

Travelers who want to explore China should present their original passport with the necessary visa to be able to book accommodation. You will not be allowed to get a hostel or hotel room without presenting your passport. In case you want to apply for a new visa or have your visa extended, you should stay in the same hotel where you had your accommodation booked. Otherwise, you cannot get a room under any circumstance even if you present a police receipt of consulate notice to prove that your passport has been held for visa processing.

There are different types of accommodation suited for every tourist's budget. From dormitories, shared rooms or even five star hotels, China has a lot of offers for those who want to take a tour in the country. Inns and other temporary housing offered by workers who have migrated to China are also available. However, this may not be very appealing because of its cleanliness and sanitation issues.

Finding a hotel is not difficult but finding the right one can be daunting. Most of the hotels found in cities offer everything in Chinese and very few English signs are displayed. You either get to hotel which is already closed or from one that has full booking. However, if you are willing to spend Y200 for a night in a hotel, this isn't really a big problem as luxury hotels are widely available. Searching online before going to China can help you get a prior booking. This way you are assured that you will have a place to stay the moment you arrive.

Meanwhile, you can also vie for the cheapest deals in dorms, hotels and rooms referred to as zhusu. Prices usually start from Y150 for hotels in most cities. Meanwhile, you can also get a rid on a sleeper train or sleeper bus if you are traveling overnight. If you are within a town area, you can go to the nearest train station where most of cheap hotels are located.

Before making a deal with a hotel, it is best to ask if they have hot water available all throughout the day. You can also check if the sink, toilet as well as the shower work. Take note to get accommodation away from busy streets as the noise may keep you up all night and get you waking up early the next day.

Negotiating for Hotel Prices

Travelers are often surprised that you can actually haggle on hotel prices. You can start by asking, "Zui Di Duoshuo?" which translates to how the lowest price offering could possibly be. Travelers can get discounts especially when they are booking for long days of stay.

Meanwhile, take note of the Chinese holidays as these are the dates that rates soar up. If you have been to China several times and have booked with the same hotel, you may be given a membership card. You can use this to get discounts on your next bookings especially when your visit falls on a Chinese holiday where rooms are usually difficult to get.

Having an accommodation booked online is also available. You will need your credit card to pay for your room even before your scheduled trip. Meanwhile, remember that not all establishments accept credit cards in the country. So if you are making a reservation in smaller hotels, you will need to have some cash to cover the expenses.

Other Types of Chinese Accommodations

Start off by checking hotels as these as the cheapest options you have. Hostels usually have personnels who can speak English. They can also provide with convenient transportation systems at a fairly priced rate. Some of these hotels are also clean compared to those that are even more expensive.

You can also book a dorm room which is usually located near university campuses. These are also found near places of tourist interest and can be a part of some hostels. Take note that these rooms have traditional toilets and baths. You will have to share this with your roommates and may take some time before you get used to it.

Rooms for rent or the zhusu can also be taken. These are found near restaurants, homes and near train and bus stations.

English signs advertising rooms for rent are not often found as foreigners are not officially allowed to have this type of accommodation. However, owners are mostly eager to get clients that they would take you in for cheaper price rates. If you have valuable brought along with you, booking a zhusu may not be a good idea as security can be a sketchy.

If you are having problems getting a room, head to the nearest massage parlor, spas or saunas. Most of these offer low prices and can get you accommodated from late night until noon. Usually, customers who leave before lunchtime are given 50% off. You can head to a spa at anytime of the day as this operates 24 hours. You will be provided with a locker where you can have your things stored.

Another type of accommodation is from budget hotels. Usually, they don't allow foreigners but you may be able to change their minds to accept you. This usually happens if you know how to speak even with smattering Chinese. Budget hotels are comparable to zhusus only that they are licensed to operate. The rooms are offered with attached bathrooms. Meanwhile, dorm type accommodations have shared bathrooms.

Some budget hotels are equipped with Internet connection to keep you updated online while others offer free toiletries. City budget hotels charge guests from Y80 to Y120 per night. Meanwhile, those operating in smaller cities can charge you Y25 per night.

Booking for Mid-range and Luxury Hotels

Mid-ranged hotels are bigger and more comfortable. The prices are not that expensive that can start from Y150 to more than Y300. You will have a clean, private bathroom if you book for a doubles room as well as free toiletries. You can also enjoy free breakfast while some hotels offer meal tickets at about Y10.

You can check out mid-range hotels while in the country to great deals, comfortable experience, clean toilets and a good night's rest. Hotels including JJ Inn, Rujia Home Inn, Motel 168 and 7DaysInn are great choices with prices ranging from Y150 to Y300.

Meanwhile, those who can afford a luxury stay while in China can go for five star international hotel chains. You can have a room reserved at Marriott Hotel or at Shangri-La. You can also get a room in Hyatt Hotel or from other luxury hotel competitors mostly operating within the city.

Luxury hotels offer free Internet access, spas, 24 hour room service and satellite TVs. Usually, western breakfast meals are offered in buffets. As the name suggest, the price can be very expensive. One night in Shangri-La hotel can cost you Y10,000.

Chapter V: Where To Go and What to Eat

China's rich history and culture will enable guests to a wide variety of top tourist destinations. Those who are spending their holidays in the coastal areas will enjoy more activities. Train rides are also short allowing you to enjoy the next city after you are done with the previous one.

Travelers who appreciate nature will not be disappointed as there are numerous scenic spots in China. You will be refreshed by the green scenery as well as the great environment rural, mountainous areas have to offer. Meanwhile, those who love to unravel history will find the country very interesting. The rich history of Ancient China can be very appealing that a day's trip to an ancient city would not be enough.

Heritage Sites To Visit While In China

China holds a lot of heritage sites. In fact, UNESCO has ranked it third given its long history and numerous places of historical interest. You can start by taking a trip to the infamous Great Wall of China, the country's landmark. The ancient iconic wall stretches more than 8,000 kilometers and myth has it that you can even see it from the from.

The island of Hainan has also received a large number of tourists after having been developed into a tropical paradise. Meanwhile, you can also check out the Jiushaigou Nature Reserve and take photos of giant pandas, lakes and waterfalls. Take a trip to Leshan and enjoy the magnificent sight of Buddha carvings situated near Mount Emei.

The tallest peak, Mt. Everest, is also found in China bordering Tibet and Nepal. Backpackers can unravel the historic and scared mountain of Tai. If you are seeking more adventure, head on to Tibet where majority of Tibetan culture and religion is found. You will be surprised that you seemed to have entered a different world when visiting Tibet.

Another heritage site to visit is Turpan in Xinjiang. The place offers grapes while taking a look at the Uighur culture. Don't forget to include Yungang Grottoes in your itinerary. You will find more than 51,000 Buddhist statues inside the caves of mountains.

Visiting China's Pilgrimage Sites

If you are looking for a taste of history, head on to different pilgrimage sites located mostly anywhere in the country. You can drop by Shaoshan, the hometown of Mao Zedong, or visit the first rural base of the country, Jinggangshan, after KMT's crackdown moe in 1972. You can also go to the Ruijin, where China was held a seat in the country's soviet republic. Taking a tour in Wuhan where the uprising that ended the Qing Dynasty was launched. It was also in this place that the Republic of China was established.

Furthermore, take a trip to Guangzhou where communist leaders trained in the Whampoa Military Academy.

Food, Food and More Chinese Food!

The food in China varies from one region to another making the term Chinese food simply a blanket. Before devouring a large bowl of noodles, remember the proper way of eating as you would offend the chef of a local restaurant. Take note that beef and broccoli and chow mein are not authentic Chinese cuisine. You will get odd looks from locals the moment you start asking if these are included on the menu.

The food are usually cooked right after you place your order. This will ensure that you get freshly cooked, hot meals. Street foods are also available but are not always recommended as most of these are cooked unhygienically.

Spend time learning Chinese food symbols because not all restaurants have English translations. Noodles written on the menu appear as 面, rice as 饭 while chicken is written as 鸡. Fish is written as 鱼, beef as 牛 and pork as 猪. If a menu reads simply "meat", you can assume that it has pork in it.

Most Chinese dishes are exotic that travelers tend to avoid. Ingredients including dog meat or snake are used when cooking meals deemed to taste delicious. If you're not up to eating these meals, don't worry of having confused orders. These type of foods are served in specialty restaurants that do not hide what's inside their offered dish. Generally speaking, rice is the main staple in the south, while wheat, mostly in the form of noodles, is the main staple in the north.

Regional Chinese Tastebuds

Different tastes cover the regions of the country. In Jiangsu, Shanghai and Zhejiang, tastes don't get spicy and are often sweet. They call their dishes Huaiyang cuisine and uses freshwater fish, other seafoods and pork as their base ingredients. You can enjoy steamed dumplings, thousand-layered cake, steamed buns with wild veggies, tofu noodles and crab soup dumplings for breakfast while in this region.

When in Hong Kong or Guangzhou, travelers will be able to find dishes that are not too spicy. The cuisine emphasizes seafood ingredients that are freshly cooked. Dim Sum are eaten for snacks with tea.

Meanwhile, Shandong cuisine remains to have a taste of the ancient culture. You will find it very delightful to eat prawns, squid, sea cucumbers and a wide variety of seafood cooked with ancient traditions. Unlike the other three regional tastes, Sichuan offers guests hot and spicy dishes.

Are There Fast Food Restaurants in China?

Certainly! These restaurants are budget friendly and cook light, delicious meals really fast. Cities in the country also have street food sold by vendors all throughout the street. If you want to experience street food dining, head to Snack Street in Beijing. Here you will find lots of tourists eager to get a taste from street food vendors called gai bin dong.

Bakeries are also found in the country where bread is often made sweet. Other pastries are served as snacks unlike in western countries where these are served as desserts. Meat on sticks grilled along the streets can also be bought. These are called Yang rou chuan, made from lamb, which have grown popular among tourists. Take a Jiaozi dumpling bite made from a variety of fillings and cooked either fried, boiled or steamed. Fast food restaurants also offer Mantou bread and Baozi, steamed buns with veggie fillings. China isn't China without noodles. You can buy a bowl of Lanzhou-style lamian in a small restuarant for authentic taste.

If you happen to miss home and is searching for notable western fast food chains, don't worry as China also have these. You can head to McDonald's, Pizza Hut, KFC or even Subway for burger, fries and pizza. Haagen-Dazs can also be bought in major Chinese cities including Guangzhou and Shanghai.

Displaying Etiquette Inside A Chinese Restaurant

In China, you don't use spoon and fork! This is not a surprise as the country is where chopsticks originated. Using chopsticks properly will please the locals while using them improperly may make them see you as an annoying and ill-mannered person.

Remember not to examine every dish using your chopsticks. Instead, you can do an eye check to examine a dish. Don't return the food back to the platter once you've already picked it up. Also, you have to wait for your turn to pick a dish as it is improper to cross over beneath someone else's arms to get food. Mostly, you have to wait for your turn as it is also improper to simultaneously pick food with another person.

Putting your chopsticks vertically on top of your bowl is a big NO! This can resemble burning incense sticks in a temple which means you are wishing for the death of the people around you. People also find it rude when you start drumming your bowl using chopsticks as only beggars do that.

Chapter VI: Festivals and Events

There are a lot of festivals offered in China that you should try to see. During these dates, air fares dramatically increase and most hotels get fully booked. If you are planning to visit the country on a holiday, be sure to have an advanced booking. This will save you time and money as some travel agencies offer great deals for early bookings.

China has five major holidays where streets get even more crowded and transportation gets jammed. This includes the Spring Festival or better known as the Chinese New Year Celebration happening every late January or mid-February. Then there's Qingming Festival celebrated from April 4 to 6 every year. The celebration commemorates the death of ancestors of every family resulting to cemeteries getting too crowded.

May 1 is Labor Day in China while Dragon Boat Festival is celebrated every fifth day of the lunar calendar's fifth month. The festival is often paired with eating zongzi while watching boat races. The festival also known as Duanwu Festival is the most famous tradition observed in the country. It is also included in the UNESCO World Intangible Cultural Heritage Lists.

By October, the Moon Cake Festival is celebrated where moon cakes are given as presents. This is done while people go out at night to meet and dine while staring at the full moon of harvest. The festival is also referred to as the day of reunion for most families as they go out and look at the moon when it is shining at its fullest and brightest. Meanwhile, the National Day of China is also celebrated in October where students get to spend a four to six week holiday.

Celebrating Chinese Festivals

Unlike most countries that wait until midnight of December 31st to celebrate New Year, China has their own new year celebration. It is the longest holiday in the country and is also the busiest. The festival has a rich history that dates back 4,000 years ago. It is believed that sacrifices have to be made to deities every year. In return, people would get good harvest after changes in solar terms are made. The new year celebration is also done to get families closer together as they take time off from work and visit their relatives.

Aside from the lunar new year, there are also other festivals to watch out for. Just after the new year, the Chinese people celebrates the Lantern Festival where lanterns are either flown to the river or lighted outside temple porches. The festival is also one of the most important traditional celebration in the country. It happens during the first full moon of the Chinese lunar calendar.

Unlike the Chinese New Year, most people are unable to celebrate it with their families because it is not held as a public holiday.

In Tibet, you can join the Shoton Festival in August where monks end their meditation sessions. They celebrate by eating yogurt and enjoying dramatic operas. The occasion has already attracted a lot of tourists to visit. It has been regarded to be one of the famous ethnic festivals in the country where entertainment, performances and competitions are being held.

China has also their own celebration of Valentines' Day called Double Seventh Festival. This romantic festival takes part on the 7th day of the lunar calendar's 7th month. The Chongyang Festival is celebrated mostly in October while the Winter Solstice Festival begins by third week of December.

Come See the Wonders of China!

Visiting China, eating their cuisines cooked with pride, meeting people, enjoying a diverse culture and being enthralled by scenic views are some of the expected things you can find in the country. We hope that you are able to find the answers through our travel guide to China! After getting useful tips and insights, we hope to see in China along with your family members and friends. With the rich history and tradition of the country, you are assured of a pleasant stay and memory-filled heart to take when you go home. Xingfu Zhi Lu (Happy Trip) Travelers!

Experience Everything Travel Guide Collection™

EXPERIENCE
EVERYTHING
P U B L I S H I N G

www.ingramcontent.com/pod-product-compliance
Lightning Source LLC
Chambersburg PA
CBHW071745020426
42331CB00008B/2180